Your family

Family **facts**

Did you know that there are many different kinds of families?

Today in school we talked about our families...

2

...and we saw that all of them are different, but at the same time, they are alike because all of them take care of us and love us...even if sometimes they get mad at us because we misbehave!

After that, we made drawings of our families, but they all looked different because we are all different too. One of the kids in the class even drew a picture of...
AN ELEPHANT FAMILY!

3

Good drawings!

These are the drawings we made, but there could be a lot more,
because every child in the world has a different family. And what about you?
Would you like to make a drawing of your own family?

4

A **family** reunion

Martha is an only child, but her family is very large, with parents, grandparents, uncles and aunts, cousins.... Some of them, however, live far away, and Martha only gets to see them on very special occasions, like when she has a birthday party.

Martha's dad spends little time at home because he has to travel a lot. When he has to leave, she is a little sad, but she knows he will come back in a few days. Do your parents also have to travel on business?

The elders

Martha loves it when her mom and dad tell her stories while they are looking at old pictures. She can see what her grandparents were like when they were young. Her parents did not know each other then. They belonged to two different families, the family of her maternal grandparents and that of her paternal grandparents.

8

Now all of them belong to the same family: Martha's family!
She likes spending time with her grandparents and learning
the many things they have to teach her.

9

Who does the dishes?

Martha also has a lot of aunts and uncles: they are her parents' brothers and sisters. Her mom has just one brother, but her dad has five brothers and sisters! They were a large family. Some of her aunts and uncles have children, and others don't. Can you imagine doing the dishes after a family reunion?

10

Soon Martha will have
another little cousin
because her aunt is
expecting a baby.
She has a big round belly,
like a watermelon.
They will need a bus
to travel together!

Mommy, I'm afraid!

Her mom and dad loved each other so much that they decided to have a baby... and Martha was born. When she was very little, she slept many hours a day, and since she did not know how to talk, she cried for what she wanted. What she liked best was having her parents sing her a lullaby while they cradled her.

12

When Martha was not feeling well, her parents took care of her until she was fine again.
If she was sad, they comforted her and kept her company.
When she was with them, she was not afraid of monsters!

13

Let's pretend...

Mark has a younger sister. It is fun having a sister, even when she is a nag sometimes and takes his toys from him or tears his drawings.... They fight and argue a lot, but they also love each other very much, and they usually end up playing together and laughing at the mischief they cause.

Mark and his sister
like to pretend they
are like their parents, and
for costumes they wear what
they find around the house.
They have a great time
playing like this!

15

A father for two

Johnny lives with his dad and his twin brother. Their mom died when they were very little, but they always remember her. During bedtime, their mom used to sing to them in her lovely sweet voice. They loved her so much!

16

Their dad says their neighbors are like their family, because they have loved and taken care of them since they were very little. Sometimes Emma comes to stay with them. She is their babysitter.

17

The family adds a new member

Jenny has a new little sister! The other day she and her twin cousins went to the hospital to see the new baby. She is very small, like a doll, and she moves all the time. She can't talk or draw or...do anything. But it will be fun once she is old enough to play with Jenny.

Jenny is spending a few days
at her uncle's house.
She has a great time
playing with her cousins,
but she would like
to go back home
with her parents
and baby sister!

19

What a crowd!

Charlotte's mother has gotten married for the third time,
but Charlotte was born during her mom's second marriage.

Now Charlotte has her own brothers and sisters from her mom and dad, but she also has brothers and sisters from her mom's first marriage and some from her dad's earlier marriages. It's confusing, but it's also a lot of fun!

Charlotte lives with her mother, but she often spends a few days with her father. She loves going to the movies with him...and taking a big bag of popcorn along!

21

Like father, like son

Paul's parents are blonde, with blue eyes and very fair skin.

Paul, though, has very dark hair and eyes, and his skin is golden brown.

He is like his mother because he laughs like she does.

When Paul gets mad, he wrinkles his nose like his father does.

When they adopted him, he did not know how to do those things!

Paul does not look like his parents because he was born in another country. Most people in that country have dark hair and eyes and their skin is golden brown.

23

The story of your life

Paul never met his birth parents, but they must have been very good looking and smart, just like he is. It is fun to know that the face and body of a child look like his birth parents, but his attitudes are very similar to those of the mom and dad who raised him!

24

Paul has brought pictures of his country of origin, where all his ancestors have lived. It is so much fun to learn about the story of your life!

25

Fiona, our teacher

And then...Fiona told us that when she was little she used to live in an orphanage, which is a place where children with no parents live. Her family was formed by all the other children there, as well as Brenda, Rose, Martin, and Carrie, who were like her parents because they loved and looked after her.

Sometimes Fiona felt unhappy because she had no parents, but now she is very happy because she has three wonderful children and a lot of friends.

27

A big family

Fiona has read aloud what Native Americans used to say:

"We are all part of one and the same big family, the big human family.
We are all alike: you, I, the animals in the forest, the sun, the moon,
the rivers, the seas, the trees, the air we breathe...."
After that, when we were playing, we tried to imagine
how Native Americans had lived!

28

Our teacher has explained that each of us is unique, even if we are twins. And our families are different too, but at the same time, we are all alike because we are part of the same family, the human family.

Activities

A family reunion

Would you like to make your family a very good present? Make them cookies! You only need 1/2 c (100 g) of sugar, a stick (100 g) of butter, 1 T (15 ml) of baking powder, 3 egg yolks, 1 c (200 g) of flour, raisins, and THE HELP OF AN ADULT! Put all the ingredients together in a bowl, and mix them well using a fork or spoon. When all the ingredients are well mixed, use a rolling pin to roll out the dough until it is about 1/2 inch (5 cm) thick. Use a cookie cutter to make shapes with the dough. Cookies have to be baked for about 12 minutes at 350°F (175°C), but this is something that an adult will have to do for you, because you can burn yourself if you touch the oven! Let the cookies cool, and soon you will be able to treat your family to them. They'll say that you are a great cook!

Like father, like son

Make a list of ways in which you are like your dad or mom. You can also include differences, and there will surely be many! Maybe you look more like your grandma or one of your uncles, and maybe your personality is a little like your parents', because you learn a lot of things from them. Maybe you sing very well, like your dad, or you like chocolate cake, like your mom, or.... Can you think of something that you do just like your father or your mother?

Who does the dishes?

Have you ever noticed who does what at home? Normally, in every family each member is in charge of a different chore, because everything works out better this way. Copy the following list and complete it with the name of the person in charge of the specific chore. You can make this list as long as you wish. By the way, do you help with the housework?

Do the dishes . . . .

Take out the garbage . . . .

Give you a bath . . . .

Hang pictures . . . .

Fix dinner . . . .

Set the table . . . .

Fix faucets . . . .

Sweep and mop the floor . . . .

Take you to school . . . .

Pick up your toys . . . .

Dust the furniture . . . .

Paint the walls . . . .

Fix lunch . . . .

Put up shelves . . . .

Do the laundry . . . .

Buy food . . . .

Make the beds . . . .

Fix the car . . . .

31

Once upon a time...

Have you ever made up a story? Would you like to try? Start by drawing a family, their house.... Do they live in a city or in the woods? Are they happy or angry? You can make as many drawings as you wish, and if you already know how to write, you can explain what is going on in each drawing. If you have brothers and sisters or cousins, each one of you can make up a story, and then you can exchange them.

When you are done, tell your mom and dad the story that you have made up. They'll love it!

The shopping list

If you did the grocery shopping, your shopping list would surely be different from the one an adult would make. Think what you would like to have for breakfast, lunch, and dinner. Write everything down on a piece of paper, or ask someone to write it for you. Then show your list to the person who usually does the shopping. Do both lists match? Maybe quite a few things are different. Did you remember to write down everything? Next time you go shopping, you can try saying what you all need at home: don't forget toothpaste, shampoo, light bulbs....There are so many things to remember!

A very special tree

To find out who your ancestors are, you can draw a tree like this one.
Ancestors are all those members of your family who were born before you.
They are very special people because they form part of your past history.
If you write down all their names, you will see that they look like a tree
with many branches. There you are, at the bottom of the tree!
This kind of tree is called a genealogical tree.

How about asking your parents to help you draw your genealogical tree?

Guidelines for parents

Good drawings!
You can find different kinds of families represented in the drawings, and comments can be made about similarities with and differences from your own. It is also possible to talk about families in the animal world: there are animals that live in families, like monkeys, and others that live alone from the time they are born, like fish.

The elders
It is necessary to explain the meaning of paternal and maternal grandparents. Your paternal grandparents are your father's parents, and your maternal grandparents are your mother's. Explain how each family lived back when they were two individual families, what the differences and similarities were, and what life was like then. This chapter is adequate for talking about the experiences grandparents have accumulated, emphasizing the fact that they know a lot of things because they have lived a long time.

Mommy, I'm afraid!
This part can be linked to a discussion with your child about birth. There are many ways to be conceived. There are parents who have had to seek medical help to have a baby, like fertility treatments or artificial insemination. The

information can be adapted to your child's circumstances.

It is also adequate for talking about newborns. Some newborn babies cry a lot and others are very quiet. Some have a lot of hair and others seem bald. Newborn babies cannot eat because they have no teeth, so they have to drink milk from their mothers or from a bottle. What they like best is to have their parents take care of them, sing them songs, and cradle them in their arms.... Refer to newborn babies your children know, and tell them what they were like when they themselves were little babies.

A father for two
After a certain age, children start acknowledging the subject of death, even when they have not had a related experience. Death appears in tales, films, school conversations.... This section facilitates talking about related doubts a child may have. Try to make your children consider death as something natural, although you should not bring up the subject but rather be open to any questions they may ask. If somebody in the family has died, especially if it is a person very close to your child, you can refer to this in making the point that other children find themselves in the same situation, and that it is normal to miss that person you love who is no longer here. It is good to talk about death whenever your child brings up the subject, so he/she can see that even when you are sad, you can talk about the person openly, remembering the good moments together. The most important thing to remember is that your children must clearly understand that they can freely express how they feel in front of you.

This subject can also be dealt with in other sections, due to the ambiguity of the drawings, and adapted to the needs the child has. For example, in the part called "A family reunion," you can say Martha never met her paternal grandfather because he died before she was born.

A father for two: twins
Twins are two offspring that were together inside their mother's belly. They can be identical, if they are exactly alike, or not. They can even be a boy and a girl who do not look alike at all. Even when identical twins have bodies and faces that look exactly alike, their personalities can be very different. Over time, identical twins can become different enough so people can tell them apart. Children can be told that some twins play the practical joke of pretending they are "the other one" by interchanging their clothes.

What a crowd!
This section, purposely confusing, highlights the complex relations we can find in one family. The younger children can be told that Charlotte has a lot of grandparents. They include not only the respective parents of her own biological parents, but also the parents of the different husbands her mom has had, who are not really her grandparents but act as if they were. The same applies to uncles/aunts and their children, who will be her uncles/aunts and cousins even when they are not related to her by birth. The important fact is that Charlotte lives with her mom and her stepfather (her mom's present husband). Her stepfather's children, who are not related to her by birth, are her stepbrothers and stepsisters.

A child should be told only that which is of concern to him/her. Even when expressions such as stepfather/mother and stepbrother/sister are more accurate, many families would rather use just father/mother or brother/sister without placing any importance on the relations by birth, since very often the personal concept of family is more connected to love than to biology.

Like father, like son
This section refers to adoption, international or not. Parents should explain that some birth parents cannot take care of their children, and that's why they put them up for adoption by parents who really can and are willing to do it.

It is important that children clearly understand that their true parents are those who take care of them as well as love them. It is also important to speak of their birth parents with a lot of respect, because they have given them the gift of life, and thanks to that, you as adoptive parents have been able to have a wonderful child. If your child is adopted, you should be open to the questions he/she may ask and give the answers the child is prepared to receive.

35